Great Business English

Phrases, Verbs and Vocabulary for Speaking Fluent English

By

Hilary Moore PhD, MBA

Diversity
Publishing

Published by:

Diversity Publishing
Diversity Publishing is a trade name of Hilary Moore Consultancy Ltd.
15D Queensthorpe Road
SE264PJ
London
United Kingdom
Website: greatbusinessenglish.com

GO TO

www.greatbusinessenglish.com

and use this code:

BOOKBUYER0701

for your 20% discount on recordings that will give you additional help with this book.

Acknowledgements

The inspiration for this book has come, above all, from my six years as an English for Business and communications trainer for Canning (www.canning.co.uk) – industry leaders in international business communication. At Canning, I was surrounded by colleagues whose passion for excellence, for helping their clients, for language and communications was, and remains, exceptional. Much of what I know about language and communications come from them. I would like to particularly thank colleagues Richard Pooley, Murray Robertson, Chris Fox, Cressida Hulme, Nina Clarke, Elizabeth Bawdon, Michael Norris, Andrew Ure, Judi Carne-White, Roz Winter-Bee, John Mattock, and Mark Hayward for their advice, encouragement and active help. I also want to thank Cassie Fox of schmublishing.com for her expert advice about the publishing process.

I am deeply grateful to Cass Business School for their support and funding through my MBA. They offered a superb programme which equipped me with the knowledge, confidence and business contacts to move forward with this and other business projects.

Last and most importantly, my family and friends have – as always – sacrificed, supported, consulted, proof-read, edited, and baby-sat - all to help me write this book. In particular my husband, Nathaniel, my parents Judith and Finlay and my wonderful friend Tami Laughlin have been invaluable help – thank you! A special and final mention goes to my brother, Chris Moore, who gave his time very generously to create the accompanying website for this book:
www.greatbussinessenglish.com.
Check it out – you'll be impressed with his skills!

Table of Contents

How to use this book

Quick Start:

- Look at the index to choose a section to study
- Read the key sentence in one of the exercises
- Practise the alternative phrases to make new sentences
- Buy and use the partner CDs to help you pronounce the phrases fluently. They are available from greatbusinessenglish.com. Go back two pages for the discount code that comes with this book.

Example:

Q: What were the sales last month?

What	were	the sales	last month?
		the costs	last week?
	was	the turnover	last year?
		the profit	

Some of the sentences you can make:

What were the costs last week?

What were the sales last year?

What was the turnover last year?

What was the profit last year?

Detailed Instructions

➢ The book is split into different topics so that you can find the language you need.

➢ Each key sentence gives you choices for building new sentences.

➢ Dotted lines separate some of the choices. By staying above or below the dotted line, you will have correct sentences.

➢ Having several choices for each phrase helps you to:
  o practise through repetition.
  o understand the structure of the sentence.
  o realise how to change the sentence to meet your needs.

➢ You will maximise progress by saying out loud all the phrase repetitions – first looking at the text, and then without looking.

➢ There are useful lists of business nouns and business verbs at the end of the book. Common meanings are given for these words.

➢ The CDs for this book are available from greatbusinessenglish.com. These will help you activate the phrases so you can use them under pressure in your job.

Visit

www.greatbusinessenglish.com

for further English learning resources.

TALKING ABOUT RESULTS

"He certainly knows how to make cold
statistics come to life."

Q: What were the sales last month?

What	were	the sales	last month?
		the costs	last week?
	was	the turnover	last year?
		the profit	

A: The sales were four hundred euros last month.

The sales	were	4	hundred	euros	last month.
The costs		5	thousand	dollars	last week.
The turnover	was	6	million	pounds	last year.
The profit					

A: The forecast for July is forty thousand euros.

The forecast	for	July	is	40,000 euros.
Projected profit		next month		
Projected costs		2013	are	
Projected sales		the third quarter		

What happened to the sales in September?

What happened to	the sales	in September?
	profits	last year?
	the turnover	in the third quarter?
	the error levels	
	the cost of raw materials	
	interest rates	
	customer complaints	

Sales went up in September.

Sales	went up	in September.
Profits	increased	last year.
Turnover	stayed the same	in the third quarter.
Error levels	went down	
Raw material costs	fell	
Interest rates	peaked	
Customer complaints		

How much did sales go up by in September?

How much did	sales	go up	by	in September?
	profits	increase		last year?
	turnover	go down		last quarter?
	error levels	fall		
	raw material costs			
	interest rates			
	customer complaints			

Sales went up by 5 per cent in September.

Sales	went up	by 5 per cent	in September.
Profits	increased	slightly	last year.
Turnover	went down	significantly	in the third quarter.
Error levels	fell		
Raw material costs			
Interest rates			
Customer complaints			

Why did sales go up in September?

Why did	sales	go up	in September?
	profits	increase	last year?
	turnover	go down	in the third quarter?
	error levels	fall	
	raw material costs		
	interest rates		
	customer complaints		
	borrowing costs		
	the share price		

Sales went up because of our advertising campaign.

Sales	went up	because of	our advertising campaign.
Profits	increased	due to	better customer service.
Turnover		as a result of	growth in the economy.
Earnings			the new product launch.

Sales went down because of the financial crisis.

Sales	went down	because of	the financial crisis.
Profits	fell	due to	unfavourable exchange rates.
Turnover		as a result of	our competitor's product launch.
Earnings			the recession.

A: What per cent of the sales are from Italy?

What	per cent	of the	sales	are from	Italy?
	proportion		profits		software products?
How	much		costs		

A: 15 per cent of the sales are from Italy.

15 per cent	of the	sales	are from	Italy.
A third		profits		software products.
A large proportion		costs		
15 Million				

Q: Did we meet the target in September?

Did	we	meet	the	target	in September?
	they	beat		budget	last year?
	you	exceed		forecast	in the third quarter?
		miss			

A: We met the target in September.

We	met	the	target	in September.
They	beat		budget	last year.
You	exceeded		forecast	in the third quarter.
	missed			

Q: How much did we beat the target by?

How much did	we	beat	the	target	by	in September?
	they	exceed		budget		last year?
	you	miss		forecast		last quarter?

A: We beat the target by 10 per cent in September.

We	beat	the target	by	5 per cent	in September.
They	exceeded	the budget		£3000	last year.
You	missed	the forecast		$40,000	in the first quarter.
				a lot	

Q: What is the forecast for next quarter?

What	is	the forecast	for	next quarter?
		the projected profit		next month?
		budget		January?
	are	the projected costs		2013?
		the projected sales		

A: The forecast for the next quarter is forty thousand euro.

The forecast	for	the next quarter	is	40,000 Euro.
Projected profit		next month		
Projected costs		January	are	
Projected sales		2013		

Q: Are we going to meet the target next quarter?

Are	we	going to	meet	the	target	next quarter?
	you	expecting to	beat		budget	next month?
	they		exceed		forecast	in January?
			miss			in 2013?

A: We are not going to meet the target.

We	are not	going to	meet	the	target	next quarter.
They	are	expecting to	beat		budget	next month.
			exceed		forecast	in January.
			miss			in 2013.

TALKING ABOUT TIME

Q: When do you expect to finish the project?

When do	we	expect	to	finish	the project?
	they	hope		start	the test phase?
	you	aim			the reorganisation?
		need			the production?

A: We expect to finish the project by March 15th.

We	expect	to	finish	the project	by March 15th.
They	hope		start	the test phase	in February.
	aim			the reorganisation	in mid 2013.
	need			the production	

Q: When are we due to finish the project?

When are	we	due	to	finish	the project?
	they	expected		start	the test phase?
	you	scheduled			the reorganisation?
		supposed			the production?

A: We are due to finish the project by May 1st.

We are	due	to	finish	the project	by May 1st.
They're	expected		start	the test phase	in February.
I am	scheduled			reorganising	in mid 2013.
	supposed			the production	

Q: How long is it going to take?

How long	is	it	going to take?
		the project	
		the change.	
	are	they	
		the changes	
		the tests	

A: It is going to take 3 weeks.

It	is	going to take	3	weeks.
The project			4	days.
The change			5	hours.
They	are			months.
The changes				
The tests				

Q: Are we on schedule?

Are	we	on	schedule?
	they		time?
	you		
Is	the project		
	the IT roll-out		
	the delivery		

16

A: We are behind schedule.

We	are	behind	schedule.
They		on	
The project	is	ahead of	
The IT roll-out			

Q: How far behind schedule are we?

How far	behind schedule	are	we?
	ahead of schedule		they?
			you?
		is	the project?
			the IT roll-out?
			the delivery?

A: We are three weeks behind schedule.

We	are	three weeks	behind	schedule.
They		two months	ahead of	
You		a long way		
The project	is	a little		
The IT roll-out				
The delivery				

Q: Can we postpone the launch to next month?

Can we	postpone	the launch	to	next month?
We need to	move	the meeting		next week.
I'd like to	bring forward	the presentation		Tuesday.
Let's		the kick-off meeting		February

We need to extend the contract by a month.

We need to	extend	the contract	by	a month.
I'd like to	shorten	the project		a week.
Let's		the test phase		an hour.
		the meeting		

CONTROLLING A MEETING

"There's no way we can come to a decision,
the meeting has only lasted half an hour."

Good morning everyone, thank you for coming.

Good morning	everyone, thank you for	coming.
Good afternoon		being here.
Hello		

As you know, we're here to discuss the new appraisal system.

As you know, we're here to	discuss	the new appraisal system.
	talk about	the policy change.
	decide	the upcoming merger.
	finalise	next year's forecast.

We have about an hour for this meeting. Is that OK for everyone?

We have	about an hour	for this meeting. Is that ok for everyone?
	until 3pm	
	thirty minutes	

Does everyone have an agenda?

Does everyone have	an agenda?
	the necessary documents?
	a copy of the slides?

Could someone take the minutes?

Could someone	take the minutes?
	make some notes?
	keep a record of decisions and action points?

Let's go around the table and introduce ourselves.

Let's go around the table and	introduce ourselves.
	hear everyone's opinion.

I'd like to have a free discussion.

I'd like to have a	free discussion.
Let's have a	brainstorming session.
	structured discussion.
	clear decision within an hour.
	clear solution by the end of the meeting.
	confirmed action plan as soon as possible.

I'd like to have a clear decision by the end of the meeting.

I'd like to have	a clear decision	by the end of the meeting.
Let's have	a clear solution	within the next two hours.
We need	a concrete action plan	before 5 o'clock.
	three new ideas	

Let's start with a project update.

Let's start with	a project update.
	item 1.
	an overview of the results.

Can we focus on the budget?

Can we	focus on	the budget.
We need to	concentrate on	the question of finance.
Let's	look at	the issue of timing.
	get back to	

Can we move on to the next topic?

Can we	move on to	the next topic.
We need to		the question of finance.
Let's		the issue of timing.

I'm sorry, this isn't getting us anywhere.

I'm sorry, this isn't	getting us anywhere.
	helping.
	a good use of our time.

We're running out of time.

I'm sorry, we	are running out of time.
	are short of time.
	need to move on.

I'm sorry, I didn't catch that. Could you repeat it?

I'm sorry, I didn't	catch	that. Could you	repeat it?
	hear		say it again?
	follow		rephrase it?
			speak up?
			slow down?
			explain it again?

So, to summarise, we've decided the forecast for next year.

So, to summarise	we've decided	the forecast for next year.
	we've confirmed	our new pricing structure.
	we've finalised	our action plan.

We're going to meet next Tuesday. Ok?

We're going to	meet	next Tuesday.	Ok?
I'm going to	confirm the minutes	before next week.	
You're going to	check the analysis	before we publish.	

Thanks for coming. I think this was a useful meeting.

Thanks for	coming.	I think	this was a useful meeting.
	your ideas.		we've achieved a lot.
	being here.		we've made progress.

PROJECT MANAGEMENT

"Harry, I want you to complete this project as quickly as you can. Give it the same speed you give to leaving the office at five o' clock."

So, let me give you an overview of the project.

So, let me	give you an overview of the project.
	update you.
	tell you where we are.
	fill you in on our progress.

So far, we have finalised the needs.

So far, To date,	we have	finalised the needs.
		chosen our contractors.
		finished the design phase.
		stayed on budget.
		stayed on schedule.
		met our deadlines.
		had some problems.
		not been able to move to the test phase.
		failed to find a solution.
		been working over budget.

A: The launch went better than we expected.

The launch	went better	than we expected.
The consultation	took longer	
The negotiation	was easier	
The testing phase	was more difficult	

We were delayed by software difficulties.

We were	delayed by	software difficulties.
	held back by	legal requirements.
	hampered by	red tape.
	helped by	the sales team.
		good customer data.

25

At the moment, we are finishing the design phase.

At the moment,	we are	finishing the design phase
Currently,		choosing our contractors.
		finalising the specifications.
		staying on budget.
		staying on schedule.
		meeting our deadlines.
		making good progress
		having some problems.
		struggling to stay on budget.
		struggling to stay on schedule.

Next, we need to roll out the software.

Next,	we need to	roll out the software.
Next month,	we are going to	get feedback from the subsidiaries.
For the next step,	we plan to	implement the system.
In the next week,	we want to	pilot the system in a team.
		get buy-in from the CEO.
		announce the changes.

After finishing the test, we'll roll out the software.

After	finishing the tests	we'll	roll out the software.
	talking to the boss		get feedback from the subsidiaries.
	getting the go-ahead		implement the system.
	completing the check		launch the product.

Q: Who is responsible for getting feedback?

Who is	responsible for	getting feedback?
	in charge of	piloting the system?
		analysing the results?
		the roll-out?
		the launch?

A: I am responsible for getting feedback.

I am	responsible for	getting feedback.
She is	in charge of	piloting the system.
They are		analysing the results.
Mr Ungaro is		the roll-out.
The marketing team is		the launch.

Q: Who's on the team for piloting the system?

Who's	on the team for	piloting the system?
	taking part in	getting the feedback?
		analysing the results?
		the roll-out?
		the launch?

A: I am on the team for getting feedback.

I am	on the team for	getting feedback.
She is	taking part in	piloting the system.
They are		analysing the results.
Mr Ungaro is		the roll-out.
The marketing team is		the launch.

Q: How much is it going to cost?

How much	is	it	going to cost?
		the project	
		the change	
	are	they	
		the changes	
		the machines	

A: It's going to cost five hundred euros.

	is	going to cost	five	hundred	euros.
It		going to save	several	thousand	dollars.
The project			a few	million	pounds.
The change					
They	are				
The changes					
The machines					

Q: How long is it going to take?

How long	is	it	going to take?
		the project	
		the change	
	are	they	
		the changes	
		the tests	

A: It is going to take three weeks.

It	is	going to take	three	weeks.
The project			a few	days.
The next step			several	hours.
They	are			months.
The changes				
The tests				

Q: When is the test phase going to start?

When is the	test phase	going to	start?
	project		end?
	pilot		
	roll-out		

A: The test phase is going to start on March 15th.

The test phase	is going to	start	on March 15th.
The project	is scheduled to	end	in March.
The pilot	is expected to		in 2013.
The roll-out			

Q: When is the launch?

When is the	launch?
	kick-off meeting?
	announcement?
	final test?

A: The launch is at 3pm.

The launch	is	at 3pm.
The kick-off meeting		on March 15th.
The announcement		in March.
The final test		in 2013.

We are over budget, so we need to get back on budget.

We are over budget	so we need to	get back on budget.
We have spent too much		cut our costs.
Our costs have been high		make some savings.

We have made some savings, so we have some flexibility.

We have made some savings,	so we have	some flexibility.
We've under-spent,		some leeway.
Our costs have been low,		a cushion.
We are under budget,		

We are behind schedule, so we need to get back on schedule.

We are behind schedule,	so we need to	get back on schedule.
We are running late,		speed up.
Our progress has been slow,		move ahead faster.
We have been delayed,		

We are ahead of schedule, so we have some flexibility.

We are ahead of schedule,	so we have	some flexibility
Our progress has been quick,		some leeway.

NEGOTIATING

We are hoping to work with you.

We are	hoping to	work with you.
I am	keen to	hear what you have to offer
	interested in	working with you.
	looking forward to	hearing what you have to offer

Q: What kind of price were you thinking of?

What kind of	price	were you thinking of?
What sort of	delivery terms	were you hoping for?
	payment terms	were you looking for?
	volume	

Q: How much flexibility can you give me with the price?

How much	flexibility	can you give me with the	price?
	leeway	do you have with the	delivery terms?
		is there with the	payment terms?
			volume?
			deadline?

A: I'm afraid the price is non-negotiable.

I'm afraid	the price	is non-negotiable.
	the volume we need	isn't flexible.
	that factor	is out of my control.

Q: What would it take for you to bring down the price?

What would it take for you to	bring down	the price?
	reduce	the cost?
	increase	the volume?
	extend	the payment terms?
		the contract?
		the deadline?

Q: Would you consider reducing the price?

Would you consider	reducing	the price?
	bringing down	the cost?
	increasing	the volume?
	extending	the payment terms?
		the contract?
		the deadline?

A: We could reduce the price if you ordered more.

We could	reduce	the price	if	you ordered more.
	cut	the cost		you cut the price.
	raise	the volume		the price was right.
	extend	the contract		

Q: How much more could you reduce the price?

How much more could you	reduce	the price?
	bring down	the cost?
	increase	the volume?
	extend	the payment terms?
		the contract?
		the deadline?

A: We could reduce the price by 5%

We could	reduce	the price	by	five per cent.
	cut	the cost		
	raise	the volume		ten thousand.
	extend	the contract		one year.

Q: What do you think about that?

What	do you think about	that?
	is your reaction to	that proposal?
	are your thoughts on	that idea?

A: I'm afraid that price is far too high.

I'm afraid	that price is	far too high.
	the cost is	too high.
	the risk is	higher than we'd like.
		unacceptable.
		out of the question.

A: We could consider that price, if other factors were right.

We could consider	that price	if other factors were right.
	your proposal	depending on other factors.
		if you increased your volume.

I think we have a deal. Shall we shake on it?

I think we have a deal.	Shall we shake on it?
That sounds good to us.	Let's draw up the contracts next week.
So, we all agree?	I'm looking forward to working with you!

PRESENTING

"Good presentation, Mr. Midgely."

Good morning everyone. Thank you for coming.

Good morning, everyone.	Thank you for	coming.
Good afternoon.		being here.
		inviting me.

Today, I'd like to show you our results for the last quarter.

Today,	I'd like to I'm going to	show you share with you explain take you through	the results for the last quarter. our strategy for next year. our new appraisal system. our new advertising campaign.

As you'll see, the results are good overall.

As you'll see, Overall, I think you'll agree	the results are good. the strategy is ambitious and far-reaching. the new system will improve our efficiency. the new campaign is innovative and inspiring.

First, I'll take you through the sales for each division.

First, After that, Then, Finally,	I'll we'll	take you through show you talk about explain	the sales for each division. what our challenges are. why we are doing this. where we stand now. what our next steps are.

This will take about 15 minutes.

This will take I'll talk for	about 15 minutes. less than half an hour.

If you have questions, don't hesitate to interrupt me.

If you have questions,	don't hesitate to interrupt me.
	feel free to stop me.
	I'll be happy to answer them at the end.
	there will be plenty of time at the end.

Ok, let's start with the sales for each division.

Ok, let's	start with	the sales for each division.
I'd like to	talk about	what our challenges are.
We're going to	kick off with	why we are doing this.
		where we stand now.
		what our next steps are.
		what our strategy for the future is.

So, what are the challenges we face?

So,	what are the challenges we face?
	how did we do last quarter?
	how is the project going?
	where do we stand now?
	what are our next steps?
	what's the solution?
	where do we go from here?

There are three key issues I want to highlight.

There are three	key issues	I want to	highlight.
	main factors	I'd like to	draw your attention to.
	examples	I'm going to	discuss.
	challenges	we need to	emphasise.
	advantages		focus on.
	disadvantages		look at.
	risks		talk about.
	opportunities		examine.
	trends		
	opportunities		

Most importantly, we need to talk about the question of timing.

Most importantly,	we need to talk about	the question of	timing.
Above all else,	I want to highlight	the issue of	budget.
	there is		resources.
			morale.
			accuracy.
			efficiency.
			payment.
			price.

Ok, that's everything on the results.

Ok , that's everything on	the results.
OK, we've covered	the questions of efficiency.
	the budget.

Let me hand over to my colleague to address the budget.

Let me hand over to my colleague	to address	the budget.
	to talk about	that question.
		that point.

Let's now move on to the timeline.

Let's now	move on to	the timeline.
Now, I'd like to	turn to	our next steps.
Now we're going to	look at	the forecast for the coming year.
	talk about	

Are there any more questions about this section?

Are there any more	questions	about this section?
Are there any		about the budget?
Do you have any		before we move on?
		before we finish?

So, you're asking about the budget. Is that right?

So you're	asking about	the budget.	Is that right?
	challenging	the figures.	
	concerned about	the risk assessment.	

Good question. Let me explain it this way...

Good question.	Let me	explain it this way...
Interesting question.	I'll	answer you this way...
I'm sorry if I wasn't clear.		give you an example.

Have I answered your question? Would you like more detail?

Have I answered your question?	Would you like more detail?
Is that clear?	Shall I give you an example?

I'm afraid I don't know the answer to that question.

I'm afraid I don't	know the answer to that question.
	have those figures with me.

I'll be happy to send you that information later.

I'll be happy to	send you that information	later.
	talk in more depth	after the presentation.
	get those figures for you	
	work with you on that	

Thanks for listening

Thanks for	listening.
	coming.
	being here.
	your questions and ideas.

40

CHARACTERISTICS AND SKILLS

"I said at the interview I was honest and hardworking - I never said I was competent."

Q: Tell me about his skills.

Tell me about	his	skills.
Can you describe	her	potential.
		qualities.
		strengths.
		weaknesses.
		shortcomings.
		performance.

A: He is excellent at motivating the team.

He is	excellent at	motivating the team.
She is	very good at	leading.
You are	good at	detail work.
	fairly good at	seeing the big picture.
	not good at	driving change.
		managing projects.
		coordinating multiple tasks.
		analysing data.
		negotiating prices.
		resolving conflict.
		meeting deadlines.

Q: What is his approach to his career?

What is his	approach to	his	career?
What is her		her	team?
			work?

Q: How does she handle challenges?

How does	she	handle	challenges?
	he	approach	the team?
How do you think	you	deal with	pressure?
		react to	conflict?

A: He is very driven.

He is	very	driven.
She is	quite	ambitious.
You are	not very	self-disciplined.
I am	not	focussed on results.
		flexible.
		cooperative.
		independent.
		supportive.
		creative.
		innovative.
		detail-focussed.
		career-focussed.
		results-focussed.
		relationship-focussed.
		client-focussed.
		organised.
		reliable.
		trustworthy.
		passionate.
		committed.

Q: What areas do you think you need to develop further?

What areas	do you think you need	to develop further?
	does he need	improve further?
	does she need	to focus on?

A: He needs to develop more flexibility.

He	needs to develop more	flexibility.
She	lacks	team spirit.
You	need to develop more	creative instincts.
I think I	lack	drive.
		business knowledge.
		experience with SAP.

A: She needs to improve her analytical skills.

She	needs to	improve	her	analytical	skills.
He	might need to	work on	his	leadership	
You	need to	develop	your	organisational	
I	might need to		my	presenting	
				negotiating	
				language	
				communication	
				time-keeping	

GIVING AND GETTING OPINIONS

Q: What do you think about that?

What	do you think about	that?
	is your reaction to	that proposal?
	are your thoughts on	that idea?

Q: Do you agree with that?

Do you agree with	that?
	me?
	the proposal?
	these ideas?

A: I'm sorry, I don't agree with that.

I'm sorry	I don't agree with	that.
I'm afraid		you.
		that idea.

A: I'm sorry, I don't think that's right.

I'm sorry	I don't think	that's	right.
I'm afraid		you're	correct.
		those figures are	accurate.
		that forecast is	

A: Yes, I think those figures are absolutely right.

Yes, I think	those figures are	absolutely	right.
	that forecast is	probably	correct.
	that's	mostly	on the right track.
	you are	partially	

A: Yes, I completely agree with that.

Yes, I	completely	agree with	that.
	totally		you.
	mainly		that point.
	mostly		those figures.
	partially		your analysis.

A: I think that's an interesting suggestion.

I think that's a	interesting	suggestion.
	good	proposal.
	great	idea.
	practical	point.
	valid	
	weak	
	bad	

GIVING AND GETTING FEEDBACK

"According to our aptitude tests you are best suited to retirement."

Q: What did you think of my presentation?

What	do you think of	my presentation?
	are your thoughts on	my performance so far?
	is your feedback on	the report I wrote?

A: I thought your presentation was very good.

I thought / I think	your presentation was / your report is / your performance has been	very good. / very effective. / pretty good. / interesting. / a bit inconsistent. / rather weak. / very poor.

I thought	your presentation was	very good.
I think	your report is	very effective.
	your performance has been	pretty good.
		interesting.
		a bit inconsistent.
		rather weak.
		very poor.

A: Your report needs to be more focussed.

Your report	needs to be	more focussed.
Your presentation	should be	more clearly structured.
Your analysis		backed up with more data.
		more deeply researched.

Q: Can you give me an example of what you didn't like?

Can you give me an example of	what you didn't like?
Can you explain exactly	what you weren't convinced by?
	what didn't work well?
	what you thought was missing?
	what you liked?
	what worked well?
	what you thought was good?
	what you thought was effective?

A: I really liked the way you lead the team meeting.

I really liked the way you	lead the team meeting.
I was impressed by the way you	approached the problem.
I really appreciated the way you	presented the findings.
I wasn't convinced by how you	worked with the team.
I didn't really like the way you	chaired the conference call.
	talked to your team.

Q: What areas would you recommend I work on?

what	areas	would you recommend I	work on?
	aspects	do you think I should	improve?
		would you suggest I	focus on?
			approach differently?

Q: What do you think I should in the future?

What do you think I should do	in the future?
What do you suggest I do	next time?
	to improve?
	to fix things?
	to sort things out?
	to further improve?
	to get a better result?
	to deal with the situation?
	to resolve the situation?

A: I suggest you try to be a little more detailed.

I suggest you try to be	a little more	detailed.
I think you need to be	more	assertive.
Maybe you could be	much more	forceful
You should be	a little less	conservative
	less	ambitious
	much less	

A: I would like to see a significant improvement from you.

I would like to see	a significant improvement	from you.
I expect to see	better timekeeping	
I would like to get	more commitment	
We need	greater focus	
	more team spirit	
	more creative thinking	

A: Overall you are doing a great job.

Overall,	you are doing a great job.
Generally,	you are performing well.
Most of the time,	I'm very pleased with you.
Some of the time,	your reports are excellent.
Occasionally,	your presentations are very effective.

A: I hope this feedback was useful.

I hope the feedback was useful.	Keep up the good work!
I hope what I say makes sense.	We just need some adjustments.
I hope you feel I've been clear.	We just need to work on some areas.
I hope you feel I've been fair.	We have quite a lot to improve.

DEALING WITH DISAGREEMENT AND CONFLICT

"How dare you disagree with me. You've only been on the board for five years."

A: Are you sure your figures for September sales are correct?

Are you sure	your figures for	September sales	are correct?
I'm sure	your data for	indirect costs	are wrong.
I think	your numbers for	last month's profit	are out-of-date.
I'm afraid			aren't right.

A: I'd be surprised if the data is wrong, but I'll certainly check.

I'd be surprised if the data is wrong,	but I'll certainly check.
I was very careful	but anything's possible.
I'm sure that's not the case	but I'll let you know after I check.
It's possible the data is out of date.	thanks for letting me know.
The figures are just estimates.	I'll send you the precise data later.

Q: I'm really concerned about your strategy for the Middle East.

I'm really concerned about	your strategy for the Middle East.
I'm worried about	your marketing plan.
I'm not convinced by	your cost projections.
I am not happy about	the volatility of the results.
I'm not sure about	the long-term outlook.

A: I know you're worried. Tell me more about your objections.

I know you're worried	Tell me more about your objections.
I understand that.	What are your concerns exactly?
I'm sorry to hear that.	How can we address your concerns?
	What would help you get on board?
	Your support is very important.

A: I know you're worried. There *are* good reasons for doing it this way.

I know you're worried	There *are* good reasons for doing it this way.
I understand that.	There really isn't any other choice.
I'm sorry to hear that.	I'm afraid we're going ahead regardless.
	We really have to do this.

Your strategy is totally wrong-headed!

Your strategy	is	totally wrong-headed!
Your analysis	was	totally unconvincing!
Your conclusions	are	totally unsatisfactory!
Your recommendations	were	crazy!

I'm sorry. Let me explain what went wrong...

I'm sorry.	Let me explain what went wrong...
I acknowledge that.	Let me put it right.
I realise I haven't performed well.	I promise things will be better.
I know things went badly.	I'll work with you to fix it.
I apologise for the problem.	It's important we move forward now.

That is totally untrue. Let me tell you why...

That is totally untrue.	Let me tell you why....
I won't accept that.	You need to justify that or apologise.
That is out of order.	You have no evidence for that.
That is not fair.	I want you to retract that.

Everyone needs to calm down. Let's focus on the objective we have.

Everyone needs to calm down.	Let's focus on the objective we have.
Let's take a step back.	Can we go back to the facts?
Let's take a deep breath.	Why don't we take a break?
This isn't helping us.	Let's listen to one viewpoint at a time.

COMPARING OPTIONS AND CONSEQUENCES

Q: Do you think we should change suppliers?

Do you think	we should	change suppliers?
Perhaps	we need to	diversify our portfolio?
		set up in Italy?
		update the software?

A: I think it would be better to stay with the original suppliers.

I think it would be	better to	stay with the original suppliers.
It might be	safer to	maintain our position.
	cheaper to	set up in France.
	easier to	keep the old software.

The problem with that is; we'll lose money.

The problem	with that is;	we'll lose money.
The risk		quality will suffer.
The difficulty		it will cost more.
The advantage		we'll save money.

If we do that, we'll lose money.

If we do that,	we'll lose money.
If we upload the new software	quality will suffer.
if we change the system	it will cost more.
If we outsource payroll	we'll save money.

That's a better option because it will be cheaper.

That's a better	option	because it will be	cheaper.
That's a safer	choice		more efficient.
			more reliable.
			more effective.
			more profitable.
That's a weaker			more expensive.
That's a less good			more volatile.
That's a riskier			less reliable.
			less profitable.

The second option is better than the first option.

The second option	is	better than	the first option.
The new software		more expensive than	the old software.
The other supplier		more flexible than	the original supplier.
		as good as	
		as reliable as	
		as effective as	
		worse than	
		less efficient than	

I think we should go for the second option.

I think we should go for	the second option.
We should choose	the new software.
We should stick with	the original supplier.
	the original plan.

55

DISCUSSING PROBABILITY

Q: How likely is it we'll miss the deadline?

How likely is it	we'll	miss the deadline?
What are the chances	they'll	hit the target?
	you'll	lose the client?
		have another shut-down?

A: It's highly likely we'll miss the deadline.

It's	highly likely	we'll	miss the deadline.
	quite likely	they'll	hit the target.
	unlikely	you'll	lose the client.
	highly unlikely		have another shut-down.

A: There's a significant chance we'll miss the deadline.

There's a	significant	chance	we'll	miss the deadline.
	slight		they'll	hit the target.
	good		you'll	lose the client.
				have another shut-down.

Q: Can you guarantee we'll finish on time?

Can you	guarantee	we'll	finish on time?
Can we	be sure	you'll	never have a break down?
Can they	promise	they'll	pay by the 15th of March?

A: I can't guarantee I'll finish on time.

I can't	guarantee	I'll	finish on time.
We can't	be sure	we'll	never have a break down.
They can't	promise	they'll	pay by the 15th of March.

A: I assure you I'll finish on time.

I	assure you	I'll	finish on time.
We	promise	we'll	never have a break down.
They	guarantee	they'll	pay by the 15th of March.

ASKING FOR THINGS

Q: Is there any way you could send the report by Friday?

Is there any	way chance	you we they	could	send the report by Friday? extend the contract? reduce the costs further? bring down the price?

It would be great if you could finish before next week.

It would be	great useful helpful	if	you we they	could	finish before next week. extend the contract. reduce the costs further. bring down the price.

I'd really appreciate it if you could send the information quickly.

I'd really appreciate it if	you they he	could	send the information quickly. finish before next week. wait until Monday for payment.

Could you give me an answer by Wednesday?

Could	you they she	give send	me us	an answer the information the report	by Wednesday? before next week? as quickly as possible?

I'd like an answer by Wednesday.

I	would like	an answer	by Wednesday.
We	really need	the information	before next week.
		the report	as quickly as possible.

It's important that the delivery arrives on time.

It's	important that	the delivery	arrives	on time.
	vital that	the information	is sent	before next week.
		the report		as quickly as possible.

There is really no option. You have to pay before the next delivery.

There is really no option.	You	have to	pay before the next delivery.
	They		change the local system.
			accept the global policy.

GREETING A VISITOR

Greeting a new contact

Good morning. Welcome to our company!

Good morning.	Welcome to	our company.
Hello.		London.
Good afternoon.		Italy.
		the sales department.

It's good to meet you.

It's good to	meet you.
It's a pleasure to	see you again.
	put a face to a name.

Q: How are you?

How	are you?
	is your hotel?
	was your journey?

A: I'm very well, thank you. And you?

I'm	very well,	thank you.	And you?
We're	ok,		What about you?
	not bad,		Are you well?

Can I get you a coffee?

Can I get you	a coffee?
Would you like	something to drink?
	anything before we start?

Q: How are things going in your department?

How are	things	going in	your department?
	sales		your country?
How is	the economy		Japan?
	business		your company?

A: Things are going very well

Things	are	going	very well.
Sales	aren't		well.
The economy	is		
Business	isn't		

Q: Have you been to Germany before?

Have you been to	Germany	before?
	our company	
	our department	
	this conference	

Q: How well do you know Germany?

How well do you know | Germany?
| the city?
| our company?
| our department?

A: I know Germany very well.

I know | Germany | very well.
I don't know | the city | well.
| your company |
| your department |

A: I come here often but I am looking forward to learning more.

I come here | often, but I am looking forward to learning more.
I don't come here |

Q: Would you like me to recommend a restaurant?

Would you like me to recommend | a restaurant?
| a hotel?
| something to do?
| places to see?

Q: Would you like to join us for dinner after work?

Would you like to join us for	dinner	after work?
	a drink	tomorrow evening?
	a tour of the city	at the weekend?

Greeting a regular contact

Hi! Good to see you again. Come on in.

Hi!	Good to see you again.	Come on in.
Welcome back	How are you?	Take a seat.
		What can I get you?

Q: How are things going in your department?

How are	things	going in	your department?
	sales		your country?
How is	the economy		Japan?
	business		your company?
	the project		

Q: What are the latest developments at your end?

What are the latest developments	at your end?
How are things	in your country?
How is everything	in your department?
What's the news	

Q: What are your thoughts on the new policy?

What are your thoughts on	the new policy?
Where do you stand on	the election results?
What's your reaction to the	latest announcement?
	change in management structure?

Q: What do people in Spain think about the new policy?

What do people in	Spain	think about	the new policy?
	your company		the election results?
	Marketing		the latest news?
			the new structure?

Q: How do you think the policy change will impact the business?

How do you think	the policy change	will impact	the business?
	the election results	will affect	the country?
	the economy		the sales?
	the budget		our margins?
	the tax changes		

Q: What happened in your project last week?

What happened in	your project	last week?
	the meeting	on Tuesday?
	the conference call	
	the presentation	

Q: What are you expecting to happen with the business?

What are	you	expecting to happen	with the business?
What is	your department		in the project?
			to the sales?
			to our margins?

Right – I guess we should get down to business!

| Right, | I guess we should get down to business. |
| Ok, | Shall we start? |

ON THE TELEPHONE

"What we need in this organisation is more personal contact."

Caller:

Good morning. Could you put me through to Purchasing?

Good morning,	could you	put me through to	Purchasing?
Hello,		connect me to	Mr Ungaro?
Good afternoon,			Head of Sales?

Responder:

I'm afraid he's not free at the moment.

I'm afraid he's	not free	at the moment.
	in a meeting	for the next two hours.
	unavailable	until 3pm.
	out of the office	

Responder:

Would you like me to take a message?

Would you like	to leave a message?
	him to call you back?
	to call back after 3pm?

Caller:

Thank you, I'll call back later.

Thank you.	I'll call back later.
	I'll send him an email.
	Would you tell him I called?
	Would you ask him to call me back?

Caller:

Actually, it's quite urgent. Could you find him for me?

Actually, it's quite urgent.	Could you	find him for me?
Actually, it's really important.		interrupt his meeting?
		give me his mobile number?

Responder:

He's free now. I'll put you through.

He's free now.	I'll put you through.
	I'll connect you.
	Could you hold?

Caller:

Hello. I'm calling to talk about the sales report.

Hello,	I'm calling	to talk about the sales report.
Good morning,		in response to your email.
Good afternoon,		to get some information.

Caller:

Do you have a few moments to talk now?

Do you have	a few moments	to talk now?
	ten minutes	to discuss it now?

Caller:

Is now a good time, or should I call you back later?

Is now	a good time,	or should I call you back later?
	convenient,	or shall we fix another time?

I'm sorry, it's a bad line. Could you repeat that?

I'm sorry,	it's a bad line.	Could you	repeat that?
	the reception is bad.		say that again?
	there's background noise.		rephrase that?
			speak up?
			slow down?

Finishing a Call:

I think that's all. Is there anything else I can help you with?

I think that's all.	Is there anything else	I can help you with?
I think we're finished.		you'd like to ask?
		we need to discuss?
		you'd like to add?

So, you're going to send the report by Friday. Is that right?

So,	you'll send the report by Friday.	Is that right?
	you'll call back tomorrow.	Ok?
	I'll send you the contract later today.	

Thanks for your time. I look forward to hearing from you.

Thanks for	your time.	I look forward to	hearing from you.
	your help.		meeting you.
	talking.		receiving the report.

GREAT BUSINESS VOCABULARY – by concept

BUSINESS STRUCTURE

WORD	KEY MEANING	PHRASE
headquarters (HQ)	the company's main power base, where the directors and chief executive work	Most of the strategic decisions are made in our **headquarters**, in Germany.
subsidiaries	smaller organisations or companies (often in other countries) which report to the headquarters	We have seven **subsidiaries** around the world.
joint venture	when two companies work and cooperate together	We are in a **joint venture** with a Chinese company
factory	production site	Our new car model will be produced in a **factory** in the UK.
plant		I'm responsible for safety at our production **plant** near Milan.
branch	customer-facing outlet for retail businesses	Our bank has a **branch** in most towns in France.
takeover	when one company buys another company	There were a lot of bank **takeovers** during the recession.
hostile takeover	a takeover against the will of the company being bought.	The collapse of the share price made them a target for a **hostile takeover**

WORD	KEY MEANING	PHRASE
merger	when two companies join together in partnership (normally legally the same as a friendly takeover)	In the current economic climate, a **merger** was the best option for everyone.
outsourcing	moving an operation out of the company to be provided by a supplier (normally to reduce cost or to focus better on core operations)	**Outsourcing** of customer service to India is extremely common.
restructuring	changing the structure (normally to reduce costs)	There has been a lot of **restructuring** after the merger.
rationalisation	reducing costs, staff, functions, or products	We have had **rationalisation** in three departments.

FINANCE AND RESULTS

WORD	KEY MEANING	PHRASE
revenue	total money coming into the company	**Revenue** is up this year.
turnover		Our **turnover** has improved.
sales	value of goods or services sold to customers	**Sales** are down this month.
costs	money going out of the company	Our **costs** are out of control.
direct costs	costs spent directly to produce and deliver the product.	**Direct costs** include manufacturing costs.
indirect costs	all other costs (e.g.: administrative salaries)	**Indirect costs** need to be kept as low as possible.
profit	money left after costs are deducted.	Revenue is rising, but **profit** is the same as last year.
earnings		Our **earnings** depend on the time of year.
gross profit	money left after direct costs are deducted	**Gross profit** for the year is 10M.
trading profit		We have a problem with our **trading profit**.
pre-tax profit	money left before tax is paid	**Pre-tax profit** is down by 3%.
net profit	money after all costs are deducted	Our **net profit** was disappointing last year.

WORD	KEY MEANING	PHRASE
margin	profit, normally expressed as a % of revenue	the cost of raw materials is squeezing our **margins**.
forecast	results expected in the future	the **forecast** isn't good for next year.
target	plan/ objective	It's an ambitious sales **target** given the current economy.
budget	A financial plan for costs and income	We are spending too much and selling too little. We are badly off **budget.**
tax	money paid to the government	We pay more in **taxes** every year.
Corporation Tax	money paid on business profits	The UK cut its **Corporation Tax** recently.
Income Tax	money employees pay on their salaries	The top rate of **Income Tax** rose to 50% in 2010.
Capital Gains Tax	money paid on gain from investments	I paid **Capital Gains Tax** when I sold shares
VAT	money paid on purchases	We need to charge our clients **VAT**.
National Insurance	money paid for health and government benefits	We make **national insurance** contributions for all our employees.

WORD	KEY MEANING	PHRASE
tax haven	region where taxes are highly beneficial or zero	The Cayman Islands is a **tax haven**.
tax loopholes	gaps in the law which help companies avoid tax	The government are trying to close **tax loopholes**.
shares	individual parts of a company usually traded on the stock market	I advise clients on which **shares** to buy.
stock market	public market for trading shares	My company is traded on the **stock market**.
share price	price of each share	Our **share price** has fallen dramatically since 2008.
share holder	someone who owns shares in a company	Our company has three major **shareholders**.
bonds	fixed income investment in company or country	Government **bonds** are becoming riskier.
yield	% return on bonds	Greek bond **yields** were at an all-time high.
economy	overall financial situation for a country or region	The **economy** is beginning to grow again.
boom	strong growth	The last economic **boom** is a distant memory.
recession	negative growth (technically, two quarters in a row)	we are just coming out of a severe **recession**.

WORD	KEY MEANING	PHRASE
economic climate	overall economic situation or context	It's a challenging **economic climate** to operate in.
outlook	General expectation for the future	The economic **outlook** is very uncertain.
interest rate	% charged by a bank for a loan	**Interest rates** were at a record low in 2010
base rate	National-set interest rate (below commercial rate)	The Bank of England raised its **base rate** by 0.5% in September.

EMPLOYEES AND EMPLOYMENT

WORD	KEY MEANING	PHRASE
appraisal	annual meeting with manager to discuss performance and goals	I need to do **appraisals** for my team this month.
360 degree appraisal	appraisal involving all-round feedback from team, manager, colleagues, sometimes clients	My company uses a **360 degree appraisal system**.
compensation and benefits	everything given to employees by the company in exchange for work	He's responsible for **compensation and benefits** at a group level.
base salary	money paid to employee regardless of performance and results	The sales team's **base salary** is relatively low.
salary bands	ranges for salaries based on responsibility level	The company has seven **salary bands**.
performance-related pay	additional money, normally calculated precisely, based on company and individual performance.	**Performance related pay** makes up 30% of my total salary.
bonus	additional money, often not linked to specifics.	It's been a bad year – there won't be any **bonuses**!
perks	'fringe benefits' – company car, mobile phone	My i-pad and car are very nice **perks** of the job.
commission	payment made to sales people as % of total sale	The sales team earn 3% **commission** on all sales.

WORD	KEY MEANING	PHRASE
development	employees' learning and gaining of new skills	It's my job to think about my team's **development**.
promotion	when an employee is given a higher position	I am hoping for a **promotion** in the next year.
high potentials	young employees judged to be highly able and given accelerated training and career paths	She's on the programme for **high potentials** and I'm sure she'll do well.
training	short courses taken while employed to improve skills	It's definitely worth investing in language **training**.
education	formal long-term learning at school or university	His university **education** was at Harvard
work conditions	work environment, including health and safety, working hours and salary	We need to improve our employees' **work conditions.**
unions	collective organisations representing workers	The **unions** are quite powerful in Italy.
strike	when workers refuse to work due to an employment dispute	There is going to be a **strike** because of the pay freeze.
morale	the level of motivation and good feeling among employees	**morale** has been low since the takeover.
staff turnover	the percentage of employees leaving every year	**Staff turnover** has dropped because of the recession.

MARKETING AND SALES

WORD	KEY MEANING	PHRASE
customer	someone who buys from you (can be individual, for a one-off small purchase, or a company with a long-term business relationship).	The shops are busy with **customers** at Christmas time.
client	someone who buys from you (generally a long-term business relationship)	They have been a valuable **client** for several years.
key account	a particularly important client or customer	I'm responsible for three **key accounts**.
quote	a price proposal before a purchase is agreed	we didn't win the contract because our **quote** was too high.
launch	when a product first enters a market	The **launch** of the new model should help boost our sales.
marketing campaign	project-based strategy to promote a product	We have invested a lot in the **marketing campaign** for the new product.
discount	a reduction from the normal price	We are offering a **discount** to the first 100 customers.
logo	visual symbol of the company or company name	our company **logo** is on all our products.
brand	overall marketing image for a product or company	We have eleven different **brands** in our product portfolio.

WORD	KEY MEANING	PHRASE
target market	the customers the product is designed for	Our **target market** is car drivers in Italy, France and Germany
market segment	a customer type, grouped by age, gender, need, lifestyle, or other criteria	We have several **market segments**, including busy professionals and middle-income families.
market share	% of the total market for a product controlled by one company	We have 15% **market share** in the middle-income market segment.
market research	investigation into the size, nature, buying power, preferences, or opinions of the market	After extensive **market research**, we've realised that our product is seen as old-fashioned.
demand	the market's desire or need for a product or service	There is more **demand** for small cars in Europe than in America.

PROJECT MANAGING

WORD	KEY MEANING	PHRASE
budget	the amount of money available for the project	We need to be careful because we have a very tight **budget** for this project.
schedule	the time plan for the project	We are falling behind **schedule** due to the technical problems.
Gantt chart	chart showing timings for multiple tasks	We are going to have to adjust the **Gantt chart** because of the delays.
contingency	additional budget or time, in case of unexpected circumstances	The delays will force us to spend some of our **contingency**.
phase	stages of a project	The problems have mostly been in the implementation **phase**.
pilot	the 'first try' of a change, applied in a limited way in order to test its effectiveness	We should have spent more time testing during the **pilot**.
roll-out	Applying the change widely, after a successful pilot.	We shouldn't have started the **roll-out** until we were absolutely confident.

GREAT BUSINESS VERBS - by concept

CHANGING TIME, VOLUMES and QUANTITIES

VERB	KEY MEANING	PHRASE
extend extended extended	to make longer	We want to **extend** the contract.
shorten shortened shortened	to make shorter	we are going to **shorten** the pilot phase because we need to launch sooner.
cut short cut short cut short	to suddenly make shorter	I'm afraid we need to **cut short** the meeting.
put off put off put off	to postpone, normally for a significant time	We've **put off** the new purchase. We won't have the cash for at least a year.
put back put back put back	to move later	Let's **put back** the meeting to Tuesday.
bring forward brought forward brought forward	to move earlier	Can we **bring forward** the launch?
rise rose risen	when something goes up (normally a linear increase)	The price of raw materials **rose** by 4% last month.
raise raised raised	to actively increase something	our competitor **raised** his prices yesterday.

VERB	KEY MEANING	PHRASE
grow grew grown	when something increases (not just linear/ can be volume or organic)	the economy **grew** significantly last year.
fall fell fallen	when something goes down	overheads **fell** significantly in the last quarter.
reduce reduced reduced	to actively make something go down	We are trying to **reduce** our overheads.
bring down brought down brought down		Could you **bring down** that price any further?
shrink shrank shrunk	to get smaller	The economy has **shrunk** by .5% this year.
expand expanded expanded	to get larger	We are trying to **expand** our presence in Asia.
peak peaked peaked	to reach a top point	Oil prices **peaked** at $120 a barrel over the summer.
exceed exceeded exceeded	to be more than	Our costs **exceeded** the budget.

FINANCES AND RESULTS

VERB	KEY MEANING	PHRASE
buy bought bought	to purchase	We have **bought** 10 new computers.
sell sold sold	to deliver a service or product to customers for money	They **sold** us 10 new computers.
pay paid paid	to give money in exchange for a product or service	We need to **pay** the supplier 30 days after delivery.
charge charged charged	to require money in exchange for a service or product	They **charge** a lot for delivery at the weekend.
spend spent spent	to use money	We **spent** more than expected on the advertising campaign.
cost cost cost	to be an expense	The advertising campaign **cost** us more than we expected.
borrow borrowed borrowed	to take out a loan	We've **borrowed** much more than we planned this year.
lend lent lent	to give a loan	They **lent** us 200M at 5% interest.
subsidise subsidised subsidised	an organisation pays a proportion of a cost, making it more affordable for someone else.	the government **subsidises** research into green technology.

VERB	KEY MEANING	PHRASE
transfer transferred transferred	to change something from one position to another	We have **transferred** our cash holdings to an account with a higher interest rate.
control controlled controlled	to have and use power over something or someone.	We need to **control** our costs better.
miss missed missed	to be under the target	We **missed** our sales target by 5%.
fall short of fell short of fell short of		We **fell short of** our profitability target for the third quarter.
beat beat beat	to be over the target	It was a good year. We **beat** our target by $15 million.
exceed exceeded exceeded	to be more than	We are over budget, because our costs **exceeded** our forecast in September.
peak peaked peaked	to reach a top point	Oil prices **peaked** at $120 a barrel over the summer.
stabilise stabilised stabilised	to become steady	After a volatile year, oil prices are beginning to **stabilise**.

MANAGING PEOPLE and DATA

VERB	KEY MEANING	PHRASE
lead led led	to manage and inspire followers	She **leads** her team very effectively.
oversee oversaw overseen	to supervise or manage in a hands-off way.	I **oversee** the production for all product lines.
coordinate coordinated coordinated	To manage the interaction between entities/ teams/project phases/ a variety of tasks.	He is **coordinating** the software rollout for 10 subsidiaries.
chair chaired chaired	to formally lead and control a meeting	He **chaired** the meeting badly. We ran very late.
facilitate facilitated facilitated	to enable – often by providing a forum for communication, from a neutral position.	He wasn't directly involved, but he **facilitated** the meetings.
mediate mediated mediated	to help resolve conflict or miscommunication, from a neutral 'middle' point.	They are in a serious dispute. I am trying to **mediate**.
monitor monitored monitored	to observe, check, and regulate	I'm not deeply involved, but I'm **monitoring** the situation carefully.

VERB	KEY MEANING	PHRASE
ask for asked for asked for	to request, without serious pressure	They are **asking for** a new delivery schedule. Is that something we can do?
demand demanded demanded	to request with serious pressure	They are **demanding** a new delivery schedule. We don't seem to have much choice.
threaten threatened threatened	to promise negative consequences if demands are not agreed to	They are demanding a new delivery schedule. They are **threatening** to cancel the contract if we don't agree.
convince convinced convinced	to get someone to believe in an idea.	At first he didn't believe it, but the data **convinced** him.
persuade persuaded persuaded	to get someone to do what you want	I **persuaded** him to try us as a new supplier.
remind reminded reminded	to help or cause someone to remember	Your January payment is late, so I'm calling to **remind**.
guarantee guaranteed guaranteed	to promise (often with legal commitment)	We want you to **guarantee** that the software installation will be finished on time.
establish established established	to ascertain, confirm, or clarify facts.	We don't have enough information. Let's first **establish** some key information.

VERB	KEY MEANING	PHRASE
highlight highlighted highlighted	to emphasise, verbally, or with bright colours in a document	That's a key point. We should **highlight** it during the presentation.
check checked checked	make sure something is correct	I'm not convinced by these figures. Can you **check** them again?
confirm confirmed confirmed	to make something provisional into something fixed or sure.	As soon as he checked the documents, he called to **confirm** the information he had given.
fix fixed fixed	to repair, solve, or to confirm	We need to **fix** this problem. I **fixed** an appointment for Friday.
sort it out sorted it out sorted it out	to resolve a difficulty	The system is causing a lot of problems. How are we going to **sort it out**?

CONTROLLING MEETINGS and PRESENTATIONS

VERB	KEY MEANING	PHRASE
focus on focussed on focussed on	to concentrate on	The key issue is the high level of customer complaints. Can we **focus on** this for the next hour?
move on to moved on to moved on to	to change to something new	Ok, so we've decided the budget. Let's now **move on to** the timeline.
step in stepped in stepped in	to enter a discussion or situation	I'm sorry, I must **step in** here. I think we're forgetting something.
jump in jumped in jumped in	to enter a discussion or situation	Can I **jump in** here?
recap recapped recapped	to repeat key points	I think we're getting confused. Could we **recap** what we've decided so far?
sum up summed up summed up	to summarise	Ok, I think we've covered everything. Let's **sum up**.
hand over to handed over to handed over to	to pass to someone else	So, I've told you about the budget. Now I'm going to **hand over to** my colleague, who is going to explain the timeline.

EMPLOYEES and EMPLOYMENT

VERB	KEY MEANING	PHRASE
hire hired hired	to employ someone new in the company	Last year we **hired** three new sales people
bring on brought on brought on		We're going to **bring on** some temporary staff for the busy summer months.
recruit recruited recruited		Growth isn't good enough to **recruit** this year.
make redundant made redundant made redundant	to remove people from the company, for economic or restructuring reasons	They had to **make** 300 people **redundant** during the recession.
lay off laid off laid off		We are going to have to **lay off** another 100 people this year.
fire fired fired	to remove people from the company – normally because the employee is at fault	He was falsifying financial records. We **fired** him as soon as we found out.
sack sacked sacked		He underperformed for a long time. Finally, we **sacked** him.
resign resigned resigned	to decide to leave a company	He isn't happy. I think he might **resign.**

VERB	KEY MEANING	PHRASE
retire retired retired	to leave a company due to age or illness	He's turned 65. He's **retiring** next week.
promote promoted promoted	to raise someone to a higher position	She's performing very well. We should **promote** her.
transfer transferred transferred	to change someone or something from one position to another	They **transferred** him from the sales department to marketing.
delegate delegated delegated	to pass a duty to someone lower in the hierarchy	He's a micromanager and a control freak – he never **delegates** anything!
deserve deserved deserved	when your effort or investment justifies the result.	He worked extremely hard for his exam. He **deserves** to pass.
encourage encouraged encouraged	to motivate with positive feedback *or* to incentivise	Our bonus system is designed to **encourage** good teamwork.

GREAT BUSINESS VOCABULARY- alphabetical

A - B

WORD	KEY MEANING	PHRASE
appraisal	annual meeting with manager to discuss performance and goals	I need to do **appraisals** for my team this month.
360 degree appraisal	appraisal involving all-round feedback from team, manager, colleagues, sometimes clients	My company uses a **360 degree appraisal system**.
base rate	National-set interest rate (below commercial rate)	The Bank of England raised its **base rate** by 0.5% in September.
base salary	money paid to employee regardless of performance and results	The sales team's **base salary** is relatively low.
bonds	fixed income investment in company or country	Government **bonds** are becoming riskier.
bonus	additional money, often not linked to specifics.	It's been a bad year – there won't be any **bonuses**!
boom	strong growth	The last economic **boom** is a distant memory.
branch	customer-facing outlet for retail businesses	Our bank has a **branch** in most towns in France.
budget	A financial plan for costs and income	We are spending too much and selling too little. We are badly off budget.

WORD	KEY MEANING	PHRASE
Capital Gains Tax	money paid on gain from investments	I paid **Capital Gains tax** on the shares I sold.
commission	payment made to sales people as % of total sale	The sales team earn 3% **commission** on all sales.
compensation and benefits	everything given to employees by the company in exchange for work	He's responsible for **compensation and benefits** in France.
Corporation Tax	money paid on business profits	The UK cut its **Corporation Tax** recently.
costs	money going out of the company	Our **costs** are out of control.
demand	the market's desire or need for a product or service	**Demand** for small cars is greater in Europe than in the US.
development	employees' learning and gaining of new skills	It's my job to think about my team's **development**.
direct costs	costs spent directly to produce and deliver the product or service.	**Direct costs** include manufacturing costs.
earnings	money left after costs are deducted	Our **earnings** depend on the time of year.
economic climate	overall economic situation or context	It's a challenging **economic climate** to operate in.
economy	overall financial situation for a country or region	The **economy** is beginning to grow.
education	formal long-term learning at school or university	His **education** is from Harvard.

WORD	KEY MEANING	PHRASE
factory	production site	Our new car model will be produced in a **factory** in the UK.
forecast	results expected in the future	the forecast isn't good for next year.
gross profit	money left after direct costs are deducted	Gross profit for the year is 10M.
headquarters (HQ)	the company's main base of formal power, where the directors and chief executive work	Most of the strategic decisions are made in our **headquarters**, in Germany.
high potentials	young employees judged to be highly able and given accelerated training and career paths	She's on the programme for **high potentials** and I'm sure she'll do well.
hostile takeover	a takeover against the will of the company being bought.	The collapse of the share price made them targets for a **hostile takeover.**
indirect costs	all costs not directly related to producing and selling a product or service (e.g.: administrative salaries)	**Indirect costs** need to be kept as low as possible.
Income Tax	money employees pay on their salaries	The top rate of Income Tax is 50%.
interest rate	% charged by a bank for a loan	**Interest rates** were at a record low in 2010
joint venture	when two companies work and cooperate together	We are in a **joint venture** with a Chinese company

WORD	KEY MEANING	PHRASE
margin	profit, normally expressed as a % of revenue	the cost of raw materials is squeezing our margins.
merger	when two companies join together in partnership (normally legally the same as a friendly takeover)	In the current economic climate, a **merger** was the best option for everyone.
morale	the level of motivation and good feeling among employees	**morale** has been low since the takeover.
National Insurance	money paid for health and government benefits	We make National Insurance contributions for all our employees.
net profit	money after all costs are deducted	our **net profit** was disappointing last year.
outlook	General expectation for the future	The economic **outlook** is very uncertain.
outsourcing	moving an operation out of the company to be provided by a supplier (normally to reduce cost or to focus better on core operations)	**Outsourcing** of customer service to India is extremely common.
performance-related pay	additional money, normally calculated precisely, based on company and individual performance.	**Performance related pay** makes up 30% of my total salary.
perks	'fringe benefits' – company car, mobile phone	My i-pad and car are very nice **perks** of the job.

WORD	KEY MEANING	PHRASE
plant	manufacturing site	I'm responsible for safety at our production **plant** near Milan.
pre-tax profit	money left before tax is paid	**pre-tax profit** is down by 3%.
profit	money left after costs are deducted.	Revenue is rising, but **profit** is the same as last year.
promotion	when an employee is given a higher position	I am hoping for a **promotion** in the next year.
rationalisation	reducing costs, staff, functions, or products	We have had **rationalisation** in three departments.
recession	negative growth (technically, two quarters in a row)	We are just coming out of a severe **recession**.
restructuring	changing the structure (normally to reduce costs)	There has been a lot of **restructuring** after the merger.
revenue	total money coming into the company	**Revenue** is up this year.
salary bands	ranges for salaries based on responsibility level	The company has seven **salary bands**.
sales	total money coming into the company from selling	**Sales** are going well.
share	individual part of a company that can be traded	I advise clients on which **shares** to buy.
share holder	someone who owns shares in a company	Our company has three major **shareholders**.

WORD	KEY MEANING	PHRASE
share price	price of each share	Our **share price** has fallen dramatically since 2008.
staff turnover	the percentage of employees leaving every year	**Staff turnover** has dropped because of the recession.
stock market	public market for trading shares	My company is traded on the **stock market.**
strike	when workers refuse to work due to an employment dispute	There is going to be a **strike** because of the pay freeze.
subsidiaries	smaller organisations or companies which report to the headquarters	we have seven **subsidiaries** around the world.
takeover	when one company buys another company	There were a lot of bank **takeovers** during the recession.
target	plan/ objective	It's an ambitious **target** given the current economy.
tax	money paid to the government	We pay more in **taxes** every year.
tax haven	region where taxes are highly beneficial or zero	Grand Cayman is a **tax haven**.
tax loopholes	gaps in the law which help companies avoid tax	The government are trying to close **tax loopholes**.
trading profit	profit left after direct costs are deducted	We have a problem with our **trading profit**.

WORD	KEY MEANING	PHRASE
training	short courses taken while employed to improve skills	It's definitely worth investing in language **training**.
turnover	total money coming into the company	Our **turnover** has improved.
unions	collective organisations representing workers	The **unions** are quite powerful in Italy.
VAT	money paid on purchases	We need to charge our clients **VAT**.
work conditions	work environment, including health and safety, working hours and salary	We need to improve our employees' **work conditions.**
yield	% return on bonds	Greek bond yields were at an all-time high.

GREAT BUSINESS VERBS - alphabetical

VERB	KEY MEANING	PHRASE
ask for asked for asked for	to request, without serious pressure	They are **asking for** a new delivery schedule. Is that something we can do?
beat beat beat	to be over the target	It was a good year. We **beat** our target by $15 million.
borrow borrowed borrowed	to take out a loan	We've **borrowed** much more than we planned this year.
bring down brought down brought down	to actively make something go down	Could you **bring down** that price any further?
bring forward brought forward brought forward	to move earlier	Can we **bring forward** the launch?
bring on brought on brought on	to introduce someone new into the company or team	We're going to **bring on** some temporary staff for the busy summer months.
buy bought bought	to purchase	We have **bought** 10 new computers.
chair chaired chaired	to formally lead and control a meeting	He **chaired** the meeting badly. We ran very late.

VERB	KEY MEANING	PHRASE
charge charged charged	to require money in exchange for a service or product	They **charge** a lot for delivery at the weekend.
check checked checked	make sure something is correct	I'm not convinced by these figures. Can you **check** them again?
confirm confirmed confirmed	to make something provisional fixed or sure.	As soon as he checked the documents, he called to **confirm** the information he had given.
control controlled controlled	to have and use power over something or someone.	We need to **control** our costs better.
convince convinced convinced	to get someone to believe in an idea.	At first he didn't believe it, but the data **convinced** him.
coordinate coordinated coordinated	To manage the interaction between entities/ teams/ a variety of tasks.	He is **coordinating** the software rollout for 10 subsidiaries.
cost cost cost	to be an expense	The advertising campaign **cost** us more than we expected.
cut short cut short cut short	to suddenly make shorter	I'm afraid we need to **cut short** the meeting.

VERB	KEY MEANING	PHRASE
delegate delegated delegated	to pass a duty to someone lower in the hierarchy	He's a micromanager and a control freak – he never **delegates** anything!
demand demanded demanded	to request with serious pressure	They are **demanding** a new delivery schedule. We don't seem to have much choice.
deserve deserved deserved	when your effort or investment justifies the result.	He worked extremely hard for his exam. He **deserves** to pass.
encourage encouraged encouraged	to motivate with positive feedback *or* to incentivise	Our bonus system is designed to **encourage** good teamwork.
establish established established	to ascertain, confirm, or clarify facts.	We don't have enough information. Let's first **establish** some key facts.
exceed exceeded exceeded	to be more than	Our costs **exceeded** the budget.
expand expanded expanded	to get larger	We are trying to **expand** our presence in Asia.
extend extended extended	to make longer	We want to **extend** the contract.

VERB	KEY MEANING	PHRASE
facilitate facilitated facilitated	to enable – often by providing a forum for communication, from a neutral position.	He wasn't directly involved, but he **facilitated** the meetings.
fall fell fallen	when something goes down	overheads **fell** significantly in the last quarter.
fall short of fell short of fell short of	to be under a target or expectation	We **fell short of** our profitability target for the third quarter.
fire fired fired	to remove people from the company – normally when they are at fault	He was falsifying financial records. We **fired** him as soon as we found out.
fix fixed fixed	to repair, solve, or to confirm	We need to **fix** this problem. **I fixed** an appointment for Friday.
focus on focussed on focussed on	to concentrate on	The key issue is the high level of customer complaints. Can we **focus on** this for the next hour?
grow grew grown	when something increases (not just linear/ can be volume or organic)	the economy **grew** significantly last year.

VERB	KEY MEANING	PHRASE
guarantee guaranteed guaranteed	to promise (often with legal commitment)	We want you to **guarantee** that the software installation will be finished on time.
hand over to handed over to handed over to	to pass to someone else	I'd like to **hand over to** my colleague, who is going to explain the timeline.
highlight highlighted highlighted	to emphasise, verbally, or with bright colours in a document	That's a key point. We should **highlight** it during the presentation.
hire hired hired	to employ someone new in the company	Last year we **hired** three new sales people
jump in jumped in jumped in	to enter a discussion or situation	Can I **jump in** here?
lay off laid off laid off	to remove someone from the company for economic or structuring reasons	We are going to have to **lay off** another 100 people this year.
lead led led	to manage and inspire followers	She **leads** her team very effectively.
lend lent lent	to give a loan	They **lent** us 200M at 5% interest.

VERB	KEY MEANING	PHRASE
make redundant made redundant made redundant	to remove people from the company, for economic or restructuring reasons	They had to **make** 300 people **redundant** during the recession.
mediate mediated mediated	to help resolve conflict from a neutral 'middle' point.	They are in a serious dispute. I am trying to **mediate**.
miss missed missed	to be under the target	We **missed** our sales target by 5%.
monitor monitored monitored	to observe, check, and regulate	I'm not deeply involved, but I'm **monitoring** the situation carefully.
move on to moved on to moved on to	to change to something new	Ok, so we've decided the budget. Let's now **move on to** the timeline.
oversee oversaw overseen	to supervise or manage in a hands-off way.	I **oversee** the production for all product lines.
pay paid paid	to give money in exchange for a product or service	We need to **pay** the supplier 30 days after delivery.
peak peaked peaked	to reach a top point	Oil prices **peaked** at $120 a barrel over the summer.

VERB	KEY MEANING	PHRASE
persuade persuaded persuaded	to get someone to do what you want	I **persuaded** him to try us as a new supplier.
promote promoted promoted	to raise someone to a higher position	She's performing very well. We should **promote** her.
put off put off put off	to postpone, normally for a significant time	We've **put off** the new purchase. We won't have the cash for at least a year.
put back put back put back	to move later	Let's **put back** the meeting to Tuesday.
raise raised raised	to actively increase something	our competitor **raised** his prices yesterday.
recap recapped recapped	to repeat key points	I think we're getting confused. Could we **recap** what we've decided?
recruit recruited recruited	To bring someone into the company	Growth isn't good enough to **recruit** this year.
reduce reduced reduced	to actively make something go down	We are trying to **reduce** our overheads.
remind reminded reminded	to help or cause someone to remember	Your January payment is late, so I'm calling to **remind**.

VERB	KEY MEANING	PHRASE
resign resigned resigned	to decide to leave a company	He isn't happy. I think he might **resign.**
retire retired retired	to leave a company due to age or illness	He's turned 65. He's **retiring** next week.
rise rose risen	when something goes up (normally a linear increase)	The price of raw materials **rose** by 4% last month.
sack sacked sacked	to remove employees from the company, normally when they are at fault	He underperformed for a long time. Finally, we **sacked** him.
sell sold sold	to deliver a service or product to customers for money	They **sold** us 10 new computers.
shorten shortened shortened	to make shorter	we are going to **shorten** the pilot phase because we need to launch sooner.
shrink shrank shrunk	to get smaller	The economy has **shrunk** by .5% this year.
sort it out sorted it out sorted it out	to resolve a difficulty	The system is causing a lot of problems. How are we going to **sort it out**?

S - Z

VERB	KEY MEANING	PHRASE
spend spent spent	to use money	We **spent** more than expected on the advertising campaign.
stabilise stabilised stabilised	to become steady	After a volatile year, oil prices are beginning to **stabilise**.
step in stepped in stepped in	to enter a discussion or situation	I'm sorry, I must **step in** here. I think we're forgetting something.
subsidise subsidised subsidised	an organisation pays a proportion of a cost, making it more affordable for someone else.	the government **subsidises** research into green technology.
sum up summed up summed up	to summarise	Ok, I think we've covered everything. Let's **sum up**.
threaten threatened threatened	to promise negative consequences if demands are not agreed to	They are demanding a new delivery schedule. They are **threatening** to cancel the contract if we don't agree.
transfer transferred transferred	to change someone or something from one position to another	We have **transferred** our cash holdings to an account with a higher interest rate.

ABOUT THE AUTHOR

Dr Hilary Moore, MBA

Hilary has a passion for helping international business people speak more confidently and effectively in English. She has many years of experience training managers from around the world in English for Business, helping them negotiate their contracts, present their results, and sell their products with more success. The training has been face-to-face and intensive, allowing her to explore deeply the language needs of business people. She has trained people in a wide range of industries – from manufacturing to hi-tech. They have come from numerous countries, including France, Germany, Italy, Spain, Japan, China, and Russia. She has also trained native speakers in communication skills and **in** the best way to communicate with international colleagues.

You can feel secure in the language she gives you, because her experience is supported by qualifications. Hilary has a CELTA certificate for teaching English to adults and also has a Master's in Business (an Executive MBA). She received distinctions for both qualifications. This makes her uniquely well placed to understand your business needs *and* your language needs.

Over the last six years, Hilary has gradually collected what she believes to be the most important language for doing business internationally. She has chosen phrases that are simple, effective and clear. She has compiled this phrasebook to be a powerful resource for English for Business students around the world.

She has also created a website where you can access recordings and other English and communication resources at www.greatbusinessenglish.com

She explains:

"Native speakers have a huge advantage in international business because they are speaking their own language. This allows them to dominate discussions, get their ideas adopted, and in the end to get promotion opportunities that others can't. On top of that, they are not always considerate towards those trying to do business in a foreign language.

I see my work as helping to overcome that unfair advantage.

This book aims to give international business people the language and confidence they need to express themselves, to participate more fully and effectively and ultimately to transform their English into a powerful tool for their career success.

Nothing makes me happier than seeing business people I've helped, achieve that jump. "

Made in the USA
Charleston, SC
19 November 2012